T0066980

The

Unwanted
Friend

Also in the **be̲i̲ng human** series:

The Lost Sun

The Flower in the Pocket

The Dragonfly in the Haze

For more information about the Being Human method, please refer to each book in the series. You will also find a video overview of the method via www.carriehayward.com/beinghuman. Further, you will find more information about the teachings in the list of resources provided at the end of this book.

The Unwanted Friend

A **being human** guide to
recognising the mind's stories

DR CARRIE HAYWARD

Illustrated by Elizabeth Szekely

EXISLE
PUBLISHING

First published 2023

Exisle Publishing Pty Ltd
PO Box 864, Chatswood, NSW 2057, Australia
226 High Street, Dunedin, 9016, New Zealand
www.exislepublishing.com

Copyright © 2023 in text: Dr Carrie Hayward
Copyright © 2023 in illustrations: Elizabeth Szekely

Carrie Hayward asserts the moral right to be identified as the author of this work.

All rights reserved. Except for short extracts for the purpose of review, no part of this book may be reproduced, stored in a retrieval system or transmitted in any form or by any means, whether electronic, mechanical, photocopying, recording or otherwise, without prior written permission from the publisher.

A CiP record for this book is available from the National Library of Australia.

ISBN 978-1-922539-90-8

Designed by Bee Creative
Typeset in Optima, 10.5pt
Printed in China

This book uses paper sourced under ISO 14001 guidelines from well-managed forests and other controlled sources.

10 9 8 7 6 5 4 3 2 1

Disclaimer

While this book is intended as a general information resource and all care has been taken in compiling the contents, neither the author nor the publisher and their distributors can be held responsible for any loss, claim or action that may arise from reliance on the information contained in this book. As each person and situation is unique, it is the responsibility of the reader to consult a qualified professional regarding their personal care.

Dr Carrie Hayward is a clinical psychologist who works with individuals to help them live more consciously and purposefully. Her training in Acceptance and Commitment Therapy (ACT) profoundly changed her approach to living, both professionally and personally.

Introduction

"

How rare and beautiful it truly is, that we exist.

—'Saturn', Sleeping At Last

Being human is truly remarkable. Our mere existence is beautiful, wondrous and mindbogglingly mysterious. But when it comes to the everyday and ordinary experience of being human, at times it can be really hard.

My years as a psychologist have taught me why — that is, the core reason as to why human beings are prone to psychological struggle. I believe this is one of the most important understandings I have learnt about the human condition.

You see, people come to see me, or any psychologist, with a vast range of struggles. Some of us struggle with depressive states or anxiety issues. For others, it may be anger concerns, eating issues, or disharmony in our relationships, and so on. And these experiences are occurring on the background of our own histories and contexts.

It is therefore easy to forget that we are all from the same species, existing together on planet Earth — all trying to navigate life the best way we can. Given our internal world feels deeply private and isolated, we often assume that our psychology is different or abnormal — that there is something wrong with us — which can make us feel alone. Like we do not belong.

Yet despite our differences, all human beings share one of the greatest dilemmas of the human condition: our innate struggle with all the things we cannot control in our lives, including the hardships that happen around us and the emotional pain that happens inside us. And this is underpinned by a core function of our humanness: our survival response. This remarkable aspect of the human condition that keeps us alive can, paradoxically, work against us when we are experiencing hardship and pain. Our hardwired need for control can typically result in a disconnect with ourselves and our core values, which disrupts our way of being with ourselves, each other and the world. And it is when we are disconnected from our values — how we want to show up in the world — that we experience the greatest distress.

In short, our psychological struggle fundamentally occurs when our *humanness* disrupts our *beingness*.

I wrote the Being Human series to explore this dilemma of the human condition. The series is informed by Acceptance and Commitment Therapy (ACT) teachings, an evidence-based framework which helps us to develop psychological flexibility in order to live a mindful, values-based and purposeful life. Put simply, the essence of practising ACT is bringing awareness, and acceptance, to the 'human' in our experience, which allows us to bring choice and meaning to the 'being' in our moments. Allowing us to live our moments, and therefore our lives, as conscious and connected human beings.

"

There is nothing more important to true growth
than realising that you are not the voice of the mind
— you are the one who hears it.

—*Michael Singer*

The Being Human series features four stories that follow the journey of interconnected characters, illuminating the different ways we experience our shared struggle of the human condition. The stories are followed by an exploration into the teaching and conclude with a practical process for you to take into your life. Each book focuses on a different teaching, and therefore can stand alone, where you will learn one helpful process at a time.

This book in your hands ——*The Unwanted Friend* — focuses on the nature of our mind, and in particular our experience of thinking; the 'voice' in our heads. Through this story, you will learn about how to consciously deal with unhelpful thinking, bringing greater connection and choice to your way of being in the world.

Each book is one piece of the Being Human puzzle. The whole series — all books connected — forms the complete Being Human method.

By reading about the story of the characters in each book, you may see some of your own experience in their challenges. And hopefully, you will discover the power of awareness around your humanness, allowing you to engage with your values and have choice over your beingness, with yourself, others and the world. This is at the heart of our purpose and meaning as human beings.

And so, welcome aboard to Being Human. I hope you have an insightful and wondrous ride.

x Carrie

The story

Wren is staring at the trail of ants as they march across the foot of the oak tree. She is staring, but not really seeing, as she avoids looking at the unopened textbook in her lap. Sheltering under the tree does not appear to have helped her concentration. Or her nerves, given her heart is pounding to the same beat as the spattering rain.

She manages to peel her gaze away from the ants and deliberates whether to attempt the first page. She looks down at her watch — there is now less than 24 hours to go. Wren sighs heavily; she has never been good at cramming in study. With each minute that passes, it feels as though her brain wants to exit the stage and shut its curtains closed. With no encore.

'Why have you done this again?' Wren mutters to herself, at the very same moment

that a streak of vibrant gold flashes
out of the corner of her eye.

Wren lifts her gaze and groans.
Across the other side of the path,
over 10 metres away, is a familiar
figure — the long golden plait, oval-
shaped face and small button nose
— standing underneath an almost
identical oak tree.

Argh, Mina's here. Wren sighs,
feeling dread, although not surprise,
to see her.

Mina, shorthand for 'Wilhelmina',
first came into Wren's life a long time ago, when Wren was in kindergarten. Boasting a
lively and outspoken nature, Mina was a source of comfort for the young and very shy
Wren. Mina had a love for storytelling, regularly captivating Wren with stories florid
with imagination, about themselves, other people and the big and uncertain world.
Enhanced by a distinctly husky voice, Mina's chatter felt endless, always managing to
fill the gaps when Wren would struggle to know what to say.

Wren pulls the hood of her rain jacket further down to cover her face. She can predict what would happen if Mina saw her: she would wave her arms vigorously, demanding Wren's attention; and she would bound over and immediately start jabbering, which would undoubtedly include her forthright opinion about the unopened textbook on Wren's lap. Wren winces and briskly shakes her head, rattling the unwanted image away.

Wren steals another glance towards her just as Mina begins to turn her head; her expression is cold, eyes narrow and eyebrows slightly raised. And the memory of the incident where Mina changed flashes to Wren's mind.

Wren can recall the day clearly, as though it were yesterday. She had been at the local park with her mother. She was playing on the swing set while her mother sat on a bench reading a book. There was another girl there too, a stranger around the same age as Wren, and they were taking turns on the swing. Each one was trying to swing higher than the other, make-believing they could reach the white and whispery clouds in the sky.

It had been Wren's turn on the wooden seat when the wind appeared to change direction. The other girl's hands pressed firmly into the small of Wren's back, with an unexpected pressure and force. Wren recalled the sense of motion slowing down, as she had lost her grip on the chains and soared off the seat. Time had then appeared to catch up, and started moving in fast forward, as gravity plummeted Wren to the dusty earth below.

A slideshow of images broadcasting what had occurred next flickers through Wren's mind: her younger self landing awkwardly on her bottom in a pile of dust and humiliation; the wooden seat, eerily empty, wobbling wildly above her head; the image of the girl running away. But it was the amplified sound of the girl's mocking laughter that was etched the loudest in Wren's memory — it had never seemed to fade, not even with the passing of time.

Wren's mother had hurried over. She scolded young Wren for being so reckless, curtly brushed the dust from Wren's dress, and then impatiently turned back to her book. Mina had then suddenly appeared. Surprised, as Wren hadn't even known she was there, Wren looked eagerly towards Mina in hope. But Mina frowned back at Wren, her face soiled with disapproval. 'You idiot,' she had snorted, as though *Wren* was the one who had failed *her*. Wren had not known what hurt her more: the pain in her leg from having landed so awkwardly, or the ache in her chest, bruised from Mina's scorn.

◎ ◎ ◎

Many years have now passed. They are still close, possibly even closer. But Wren and Mina's bond is now different. Mina has become increasingly possessive and demanding. Always telling Wren what to say and do; it feels like Mina never stops bossing her around. Typically worse at night-time when Mina stays the night, Wren finds herself lying in bed listening to Mina's endless monologue — telling her version of the events of the day. On repeat. Over and over. Wren often tries to ignore her, but the more she tries to block out Mina's voice, the noisier Mina seems to get.

Louder, and negative too; Mina's attitude is tarnished with suspicion. It is as though

Mina's ability to trust fell, all those years ago, at the same time Wren had fallen from the swing — left with a 'glass' of perspective that is now half empty. For when Wren suggests she might try something new, such as a new hobby or sport, Mina cautions against it.

You won't be good enough. Remember what happened at the park. What if nobody likes you?

Mina warns her repeatedly, convincing Wren that she is only trying to help. But sometimes Wren gets so distressed by Mina's relentless doubt, she screams at her to stop. They end up shouting at each other, each of them getting louder, desperate to drown the other out. At these times Wren can't tell whose voice belongs to whom.

Throughout the years, there have been times when Wren has tried to distance herself from Mina. And there are occasions where Mina will give Wren space, often walking away with disinterest when Wren starts talking to other people or becomes focused on what she is doing: playing sport; absorbed in her schoolwork; engrossed in her favourite TV show.

But for Wren, it feels as if there is a strong magnetic field between them, always pulling them back together again. An uncomfortable connection, yet at the same time it is comforting in its familiarity.

Just then, Mina locks eyes with Wren. She begins to walk her way. Wren starts to panic. Already worried about the important day she has tomorrow, she can't bear the thought of Mina making it harder.

I can't be around her. I have to get out of here.

Wren jumps up and hastily grabs her bike from against the tree. She jumps on and starts pedalling, and her heart and legs both start racing as though they are coaxing each other along.

Wren hurriedly cycles down a crushed gravel path that is blotched with deep puddles of rain. Her frantic pedalling is creating sprays of water around her. She is too frenzied to notice.

Wren spots a gate ahead of her and heads towards it, hoping she will be more concealed on the other side. She manages to fling it open with a push of her hand and races through, continuing to follow the pathway that now circles around a large pond.

By now the rain has ceased but is quickly replaced by a gust of wind. A bunch of vibrant orange leaves soar past Wren. Her vision is impeded by a veil of amber and she has no choice but to slow down.

As the leaves begin to find their way to the ground, Wren stops riding by planting one foot on the ground below her. She takes a moment to catch her breath and wipe away the tiny beads of sweat that have formed on her furrowed brow. She then brings her foot back to the pedal and starts to cycle again. This time more slowly.

Wren keeps following the pathway around the pond when suddenly she is startled by a high-pitched screech coming from behind.

'Wren!' the voice yells. 'Watch out!'

Wren immediately looks up to see a large tree branch, directly above her head, break away from its trunk. Fear kicks in and catches her breath as she instantly steers her bike out of the way. The branch snaps off and the edge of it bumps Wren's left shoulder, before thudding to the ground.

Wren lets out her held breath. She looks behind her, slowly, and confirms the owner of the voice.

It's her.

Mina has saved Wren from the falling branch.

Wren climbs off her bike and wheels it around. She pulls the hood of her jacket down from her head. Wren looks at Mina and smiles. A warm expression now captures Mina's face. She looks just like she used to.

'Hello Mina,' Wren says, cautiously. 'Thank you.'

Mina smiles back and walks over to Wren.

Unsure of what to do or say next, Wren slowly lays her bike on the ground and takes a few steps towards the edge of the pond. Mina follows and stands by Wren's side. Wren looks down into the stilled water and stares down at her own reflection — her oval-shaped face, button nose, long plait.

It is the only reflection in the water.

She turns her head to the side.

Mina is still there.

In the corner of Wren's mind.

As she has always been.

Wren stares at Mina now, as though she is looking at her with different eyes. Wren's memory opens up, with new memories surfacing, like a kaleidoscope of fluttering butterflies released from captivity.

Wren remembers her first day at kindergarten. Young Wren sitting in her bedroom early that morning with a pain in her stomach, all alone. She can now recall being cross-legged on the carpeted floor and squeezing her eyes tightly, making a wish. She wished, desperately, for a friend. Just for her. Wren had then opened her eyes to find Mina there. There in the front of her mind.

She recalls all the times Mina would talk her out of going somewhere, or would judge or criticize her. Wren would feel a deep sadness. And when seeing this, Mina's expression would look stunned rather than cruel. Even dejected and misunderstood. She would often plead with Wren, telling her that she was simply trying to help and would hug her so tightly that it felt as if Mina would dissolve into her arms. As though they then became one person.

And Wren recalls the incident at the park. But this time a new part of the memory comes to mind. After Mina had scolded young Wren left on the dusty earth, she eventually turned back to her and reached out her hand to help Wren up. Mina had gripped her hand tightly, as if to say *I am here*. She then softened her expression and whispered, 'I will not let that happen to you again.'

Wren now understands when it was that Mina had transitioned from the imaginary friend, originally there to comfort her, to the voice in her head that has always been there to protect her.

Wren walks back to her bike and picks it up off the ground. As she grips the rubber handlebars, she notices a small parade of tiny ants trekking from her bike onto her right hand. She notices, and enjoys, the tickling sensation on her skin. She notices

the rhythmic but imperfect unison they move in — trusting each other as they march collectively towards what they need to survive. And this time she is not just looking, but watching. While beside her, the image of Mina is no longer there.

Wren starts pedalling back through the park. She is by herself but does not feel alone; the feeling of Mina is still with her.

As it always has been.

◎ ◎ ◎

The next morning Wren is woken by the sound of a lawnmower next door. She reaches down to pick up her neglected textbook and at the same time checks the time on her bedside clock. Her stomach flutters as she realizes she has five hours before she needs to leave. At that moment, she hears a husky voice in her head:

What's the point? There's too much to learn! You will fail.

Wren pauses and considers these words. At the same time, she feels a dull ache coming from her left shoulder. She looks over and down at her shoulder and spots a purple bruise. A leftover mark from Mina having saved her; Mina being there when she needed help. *But is she helping me this time?* she questions.

No Mina, you are not helping me right now.

Wren notices a different feeling in her gut. It feels like courage.

She puts on her glasses and chooses to zoom her attention towards her textbook. She begins to read. She can hear the lawnmower outside. The clock ticking. Mina's voice. Many noises are there. But the noises are in the background while she keeps reading, with her book in the foreground.

Later that day Wren is sitting at the bus stop, waiting. She reads the final page of her textbook, before putting it away in her bag. A young man sits down next to her. She turns her eyes towards him. He looks familiar.

Wren sees an image of a golden plait flash in the corner of her eye, and the echo of a husky voice. And at the same time, she keeps her gaze towards the young man. 'What are you studying?' he asks her. They lock eyes and start talking.

Afterword

The human mind is in constant motion. As we move throughout our day, we experience an endless dialogue of thought — words and images running through our head. And we are programmed to experience the world through these thoughts. Most of this thinking happens to us — thoughts automatically come into our minds, beyond our conscious control. That is, we choose only a tiny amount of our daily thoughts. It therefore can be said that the mind has a 'mind' of its own.

One of the main functions of the mind's activity is problem solving; to control and/ or prevent anything from going wrong. Its primary job is to keep us alive so that we can reproduce and our species can continue. The mind is therefore regularly analysing our environment, on the lookout for threat.

When we are faced with immediate, life-threatening danger, this control function is very effective. For instance, in Wren's story, her mind automatically perceived threat in the falling branch, which activated her physiological fear response and triggered Wren to immediately flee from the danger. This control function of the mind was very efficient in protecting her from harm.

Part of the mind's control function is also to protect us from *potential* harm. It does this by attempting to explain and predict the world around us. The mind feels safer when the world makes sense. Therefore, when something happens to us that causes us emotional pain, our mind will draw on existing information — past experience, prior learnings and observations about the world — to create a narrative, or story, to make sense of our emotional discomfort. This induces a temporary feeling of safety in the known, rather than feeling vulnerable in the unknown, with the function of protecting us from future emotional pain.

The narratives, or stories, of the mind (also often referred to as schemas, parts or self-limiting beliefs) can take on a life of their own. They become a framework that our brains use to see the world, helping us to organize and interpret information as quickly as possible, allowing the brain to conserve energy and work more efficiently.

The stories filter the way we see the world, favouring information that fits within the story and disregarding competing information. Every time we interpret the world through these stories, they are reinforced (i.e. they become stronger), which creates a habit for our minds to think this way.

The mind is especially susceptible to creating stories around failure and rejection. This is due to our primal need to be accepted into a group for survival advantages. When another person does wrong by us (e.g. if we experience a difficult or traumatic event), we regularly make a judgment about ourselves, such as 'I am not enough', or about the other person, such as 'they can't be trusted'. This helps us explain the wrongdoing. It can take just one event, whether it be 'big' or 'small', for a story to be generated and for it to have ongoing impact.

This can be further influenced by the age we are when we experience the event. For Wren, the incident she experienced at the park — being pushed off the swing — occurred around the age when we are developmentally egocentric. That is, the age when our young minds start making meaning of ourselves, others and the world, through the viewpoint of ourselves. With difficulty in seeing all different perspectives and parts to a situation, our minds are inclined to 'personalize' other people's behaviours; this often leads to questioning ourselves, including our worth, value and 'enough-ness' when something goes wrong, thus creating a story or identity about who we are. We then buy into the story as though this is the reality and truth. It can stick with us and incessantly impact how we interpret future experiences.

The stories generate many of our everyday thoughts, often in the form of critical and distorted thinking about ourselves, others and the world. This can include disruptive ruminations about the past or worrisome thoughts about the future, which significantly affect how we feel (e.g. generating anger, anxiety, sadness, etc.) and will regularly dictate how we react.

Observing thoughts

We cannot control most of our thoughts. In fact, the more we try to stop or push away our thoughts, the 'bigger' they typically become. But we can control their impact. After all, thoughts are just words and pictures streaming through our mind. The power they have lies only in our relationship to them — essentially, how much attention we choose to give them.

When we are 'in' our thoughts (sometimes without realizing) they impact how we feel and often what we do (how we react). But when we notice our thoughts as thoughts, we begin to become an observer rather than being in the content — we start to look *at* our thoughts rather than look *from* our thoughts. And given we cannot be looking *at* our thoughts and be 'in' them at the same time, observing them therefore helps us create some distance from them. Observing our thoughts creates space.

Just like Mina in the story, it can be useful to give the voice inside our head — the automatic thinker of our thoughts — a name (i.e. 'X'). And any time that we experience an unhelpful (and often repetitive) thought — revealing the stories and habits of our mind — we can notice that it is the automatic voice we call 'X' that is thinking this way. By doing this, we are stepping into the part of us that is separate to this voice, the part of us that is always there. That is, the part of us that can notice. Which gives us space.

This space gives us choice. We want to choose whether to listen to our thoughts, based on their *helpfulness*.

You can assess the helpfulness of your thoughts by first noticing your mind ('X'); that is, notice your thoughts as thoughts. Then ask yourself three questions:

» Are these thoughts part of a story I have heard before?
» Are these thoughts helping me right now?
» Are these thoughts allowing me to be who I want to be and to do what matters?

If we decide that our thinking is not helping us, we can choose not to listen to the voice in our head. We can then bring our attention back to the present moment and choose who we want to be. We need to accept that the thoughts may still be there. But we can treat our thoughts like a voice ('X'), noise or song playing in the background while we bring our attention to what is in front of us and what we are doing, in the foreground.

In summary

Our mind is a remarkable tool. It is what makes us uniquely human. It is what allows us to wander towards meaning, and it enables progress in our world. It is what keeps us alive.

Sometimes our mind can feel like our friend. Sometimes it can feel like our enemy. And it can often make us feel as if we are the only ones who think the way we do. But our human minds are all the same in how they function: trying to control the world and how we feel, to keep us safe by trying to shield us from pain, which can, paradoxically, cause us more pain.

The key is to manage our mind rather than letting our mind manage us. All we have to do is notice. Observe when the underlying intention of our automatic thoughts, habitual narratives or stories might be to protect us from pain, but identify when it is not actually helping us in that very moment. And just like Wren, we can then choose where we want our attention to be, allowing us to come back to ourselves and the world, in any given moment.

The Being Human method

The Being Human method brings together each process presented in the four books of the Being Human series. It is a method that involves four steps for awareness and connection. The first two steps — 'hello mind' and 'hello heart' — allow us to be aware of our humanness. The second two steps — 'hello being' and 'hello world' — allow us to connect to our beingness with ourselves, our fellow humans and the physical world.

You can practise just one step or the full method, in any moment. It is particularly helpful when you are experiencing psychological distress or unhelpful distraction/disconnection.

1. Hello mind

a. Notice your thoughts — that is, what your mind is saying to you.

b. Identify whether these thoughts are a familiar 'story' that your mind has told you before. For example, your mind might be telling you thoughts around the 'I'm not good enough' story or the 'No one cares about me' story.

c. Ask yourself whether your thoughts are helping you right now.

'Hello mind. These thoughts are an old story.
They are not helping me right now.'

2. Hello heart

a. Name the feeling/sensations in your body.

b. Identify the value underneath the feeling — what is it that matters to you for this feeling to be there?

c. Allow the feeling/sensations to be there (without judging yourself or the feeling).

It can help to ground yourself by placing a hand on your heart and taking a slow, deep breath as you gently say to yourself:

> *'Hello heart. I am feeling [...]*
> *because I care about [value].*
> *And that's okay.'*

And now that you are connected to your values ...

3. Hello being

Say hello to who you want to be in the world.

    a. Check in with your values (i.e. the person you want to be) in that moment.

    b. Choose a response/behaviour in alignment with your values.

Gently say to yourself:

> *'Hello being. Who do I want to be in the world right now?'*

4. Hello world

Say hello to the world around you. Reconnect to the physical world, including nature and people around you, by connecting with your senses.

Don't just see, but watch.

Don't just hear, but listen.

Don't just touch, but feel.

Don't just smell, but inhale.

Don't just taste, but savour.

And where appropriate, bring a 'wow' to that experience.

'Hello mind. Hello heart.
Hello being. Hello world.'

Resources

General resources

Baird, J. 2020, *Phosphorescence: On awe, wonder and things that sustain you when the world goes dark*, 4th Estate.

Brown, B. 2021, *Daring Greatly: How the courage to be vulnerable transforms the way we live, love, parent, and lead,* Penguin Life.

Carlson, R. 2017, *The Sense of Wonder: A celebration of nature for parents and children*, HarperCollins Publishers.

Coates, K. and Kolkka, S. 2022, *How to Be Well: A handbook for women*, Simon & Schuster.

Goodwin, K. 2023, *Dear Digital, We Need to Talk*: *A guilt-free guide to taming your tech habits and thriving in a distracted world*, Major Street Publishing.

Hari, J. 2022, *Stolen Focus: Why you can't pay attention*. Bloomsbury.

Johnson, S. 1999, *Who Moved My Cheese? An amazing way to deal with work and your life*, Vermilion.

Katie, B. 2018, *A Mind at Home with Itself: How asking four questions can free your mind, open your heart, and turn your world*, HarperOne.

Siegel, D. J. 2016, *Mind: A journey to the heart of being human*, W.W. Norton & Company.

Siegel, D, J. 2012, *Mindsight: The new science of personal transformation*, Bantam Books.

ACT resources

Eifert, G.H., McKay, M. and Forsyth, J.P. 2006, *ACT on Life Not on Anger: The new Acceptance & Commitment Therapy guide to problem anger*, New Harbinger Publications.

Harris, R. 2016, *The Single Most Powerful Technique for Extreme Fusion*, e-book, www.actmindfully.com.au/upimages/The_Single_Most_Powerful_Technique_for_Extreme_Fusion_-_Russ_Harris_-_October_2016.pdf

Harris, R. 2021, *The Happiness Trap: Stop struggling, start living*, 2nd edition. Exisle Publishing.

Hayes, L.L., Ciarrochi, J.V. and Bailey, A. 2022, *What Makes You Stronger: How to thrive in the face of change and uncertainty using Acceptance and Commitment Therapy*, New Harbinger.

Hayes, S. 2019, *A Liberated Mind: How to pivot toward what matters*, Avery.

Hayes, S.C. and Smith, S. 2005, *Get Out of Your Mind and Into Your Life: The new Acceptance and Commitment Therapy*, New Harbinger.

Leonard-Curtain, A. and Leonard-Curtain, T. 2019, *The power of small: How to make tiny but powerful changes when everything feels too much*, Hachette.

LeJeune, J. 'Pain and value: Two sides of the same coin', https://portlandpsychotherapy.com/2012/06/pain-and-values-two-sides-same-coin-0/

Oliver, J., Hill, J. and Morris, E. 2015, *Activate Your Life: Using acceptance and mindfulness to build a life that is rich, fulfilling and fun*, Constable & Robinson.

Acknowledgments

A heartfelt thank you to the team at Exisle Publishing for giving these books a welcoming home. A particular thank you to Gareth for seeing the potential in this series and to Anouska, Karen and Enni for taking such good care of these stories.

To the very talented Lizzie Szekely — I adore working with you and am constantly dazzled by your creative mind and your beautiful illustrations. Thank you for being so dedicated to these books and for befriending the 'W' characters the way you have.

I would like to thank Virginia Lloyd for her brilliance in editing the earlier versions of this series, and for her overall support in shaping this vision.

There were a number of friends and colleagues who generously gave their time to read initial manuscripts in this series and give their feedback: Kate James, Russ Harris,

Aisling Curtain, Louise Hayes. I would also like to thank other folk within the ACBS community, for introducing me to ACT and for creating such a supportive community.

I am hugely grateful for my friends and family:

Warwick — for being a loyal cheerleader of this series. And of us.

Amber and Trinity — for your enthusiasm and support.

Ryan — for the time, care and wisdom you have given this series. Your way with the written word blows my mind.

My parents — Mum, Andrew, Dad and Chrissi — for your endless love, support, and for your devotion to your grandchildren.

Spencer, Alfie and Sullivan — you are my best little teachers of being attentive, curious and playful.

Thank you to all the human beings who have joined me in my therapy room — thank you for trusting me. Thank you for teaching me.

And finally, thank you to everyone who stepped into the first version of Winnie's world, and to those embarking on this Being Human series. I hope that reading the characters' stories helps you to normalise and choose compassion for our complex humanness, and to revel in our extraordinary world.

It really is so rare and beautiful that we even exist.